# Food and Love: Dealing with Family Attitudes About Weight

# Food and Love: Dealing with Family Attitudes About Weight

Elizabeth Frankenberger

The Rosen Publishing Group/New York

The Teen Health Library of Eating Disorder Prevention

*With love and gratitude to my mother and brother, who have always seen me through.*

*Huge thanks are due to my dear friend and editor, Michele Drohan.*

The people pictured in this book are only models. They in no way practice or endorse the activities illustrated. Captions serve only to explain the subjects of photographs and do not in any way imply a connection between the real-life models and the staged situations. News agency photos are exceptions.

Published in 1998 by the Rosen Publishing Group, Inc.
29 East 21st Street, New York, NY 10010

Copyright © 1998 by the Rosen Publishing Group, Inc.

First Edition

**Library of Congress Cataloging-in-Publication Data**

Frankenberger, Elizabeth.
    Food and love: dealing with family attitudes about weight / by Elizabeth Frankenberger.
    p. cm. — (The teen health library of eating disorder prevention)
    Includes bibliographical references and index.
    Summary: Explains the role that food plays in the home and how the family affects self-image, and provides suggestions for healthy living to protect against eating disorders.
    ISBN 0-8239-2760-1
    1. Eating disorders in adolescence—Juvenile literature. 2. Food-Psychological aspects—Juvenile literature. 3. Family—Juvenile literature. 4. Parent and child—Juvenile literature. 5. Reducing diets—Juvenile literature. [1. Eating disorders. 2. Eating customs. 3. Food—Psychological aspects. 4. Family. 5. Parent and child.] I. Title. II. Series.
RJ506.E18F73  1998
616.85'26'00835—dc21                                                                     98-16922
                                                                                          CIP
                                                                                          AC

*Manufactured in the United States of America*

# Contents

# Introduction

What do you see when you look in the mirror? Do you see a resemblance to either of your parents' faces? Do you see a body that you wish looked more like your sister's? Or do you like what you see, even if it differs from the appearance of your friends?

All people have one very simple thing in common: they entered the world from their mother's womb. Thus, everyone is the result of some form of parenting—regardless of culture, race, economic status, or other conditions. How we see ourselves often greatly depends on the kinds of values, traditions, and support our parents gave us while we were growing up. And no matter how strongly they may wish for our happiness and self-assurance, sometimes their desire for our personal success leaves us feeling pressured, depressed, guilty, or inadequate.

Occasionally, teens who feel this way take out their frustrations on their bodies because it's the one thing over which they have complete control. Roughly one-third of all teenage girls—and an increasing number of boys—in the United States will develop an unhealthy relationship with food. That can lead to serious eating disorders, such as anorexia nervosa (intentional starvation), bulimia nervosa (weight control through bingeing and purging), or binge eating disorder (when a person eats large amounts of food, but does not purge). The causes of eating disorders are complex. But many researchers recognize that family problems can be at the root of them.

*Food and Love* aims to shed some light on the subject of nourishment—both physical and emotional—in the home. Though no two families are alike, this book will help you recognize the role that food plays in your household and how it affects your self-image. It will also help you make changes in your family's food habits, if you choose to do so, without causing major problems. You will be given some suggestions for healthy living, including a few facts about good nutrition and exercise.

But, perhaps most important, you will learn to trust your feelings and communicate them to your family. Confronting family members about certain issues can be difficult, but understanding where your parents get their ideas and thoughts about food and eating will make it easier to talk to them.

If you recognize yourself or someone you love in these pages, be assured that help is available. You are not alone. There are many ways to deal with and overcome the obstacles you face.

# Understanding the Relationship Between Food and Family

We learn everything from our parents, from our own name to how to hold a fork and knife. In fact, it is the feeding ritual that creates the first bond between mother and child. Breast-milk, baby-food, paper-bag lunches, picnic baskets, birthday cakes, graduation barbecues—if you break down what most special family occasions have in common, it's food!

But food can be a complicated issue. We need to eat to live, but sometimes it's not easy to live with what we're offered to eat. If you have ever dined at a friend's house, you may know how difficult it can be to express concerns about what's going on at the table. . . .

*"Would I offend Sally's mother if I tell her I don't like fish?"*

*"Am I being rude if I don't eat the broccoli?"*

*"I'm hungry but too shy to ask for more."*

*"Why doesn't Sally's father say anything during dinner?"*

## Eating Rituals

Now, consider your own house. The answers to these questions may help you discover how much impact your family's eating rituals have on your life.

- ❑ Where do you eat? Does your family eat together every night?
- ❑ Who shops for the food? Are you told what to eat, or how to eat the food you've been given?
- ❑ Have you ever been punished and denied a meal? Have you ever been punished because you refused to eat a meal?
- ❑ Are you forced to eat foods you don't like?

❏ Do you have to eat even though you're not hungry?

As we grow older, we may begin to question the function of our family eating rituals.

*"Why do I have to wait for my brother to come home from baseball practice before I can eat dinner?"*

*"If I'm hungry while I'm doing homework, why can't I have a snack?"*

*"Benji's parents let him and his brother drink soda, so why can't I ?"*

## Learning to Eat

In the same way that every culture has its own staple food—rice in China, pasta in Italy, couscous in North Africa—each household has its own rules about how food is prepared, served, and eaten. Research has shown that young children eat according to their physical hunger. They naturally regulate their food intake and refuse even one more bite of food if they are full. But parents soon interfere with their children's eating patterns. They take control over what their children eat around the time children turn three or four. When this happens, children learn to eat for reasons other than hunger. And food takes on a different meaning.

The dinner table is often the central focus of a family's eating rituals. What happens at the table sends powerful messages about food.

You learn, at a very young age, what is okay to eat after school or what is not allowed before dinner. You may be told that candy and other sweets are "bad" for you, but you are given such foods as rewards for "good" behavior, such as finishing chores or achieving in school. With all these mixed messages about food, it can become difficult to express our own individual style and preferences for eating. Many researchers believe it's important to relearn how to eat like a child. It is the first step toward having a healthy, or normal, relationship with food.

# The Food and Weight Connection

Do your family's attitudes about food ever contribute to your own anxiety about how you look or how much you weigh? What words are spoken in your home about these issues?

*"I remember when you were just a little girl. Now you're filling out and becoming a young woman."*

*"Maybe you should start exercising. Your thighs are getting a bit chunky."*

*"My son takes after his father. With that belly, you'd think he spent his days in front of the TV with a six-pack of beer!"*

*"Have you considered going on a diet now that you're a teenager?"*

*"Don't get fat like your Aunt Sylvia!"*

Sometimes people say insensitive things to others. Many times, when your parents are trying to offer advice and guidance, they don't realize that their words can be hurtful to you. Do any of the above criticisms or questions sound familiar to you? And if so, how do you react to them?

You may develop self-destructive behavior patterns—such as starvation or overeating—as a result of these types of comments. That's why it's so important to communicate certain feelings and concerns to your family. Even though speaking up may be uncomfortable for you, this book aims to help you to do one very important thing: express yourself!

## Food-Awareness Activity

Learning about your own eating habits can help you to express your feelings about food in an intelligent and effective manner. Here's a food-awareness project for you to complete during the course of one day. All you need is a pen, a sheet of paper, and a little bit of patience!

## What Do You Eat During the Day— and Why?

Fold a piece of paper in half so that you have a two-column page. Label the left-hand column "Food Consumed" and the other, "Reason." Write down everything that you eat during the day.

For example:

| Food Consumed | Reason |
|---|---|
| cornflakes with milk | breakfast |
| mashed potatoes | school lunch |
| pasta, bread and salad | dinner |
| chocolate pudding | dessert |

Your first entries will be fairly straightforward. The point of this exercise is to determine why you eat what you do. At the end of the day, you will look at what has been consumed to gain a better understanding of how you use food to (a) feed yourself, (b) calm yourself, (c) entertain yourself, (d) treat yourself, or (e) punish yourself.

Try to limit your "Reasons" to six words or less. This will allow you to pinpoint what you're thinking about when you turn to food.

Before you wrap up your day and call it a night, refer to your food diary and answer the following questions:

1. Am I a healthy eater? Which foods are good and which are bad for my body?

2. Do I eat things away from home that aren't "allowed" in it? Why?

| Food Consumed | Reason |
| --- | --- |
| potato chips | break between classes |
| ice cream | celebrated end of final exams |
| soda and candybar | needed energy to study |
| two rice cakes | felt guilty about the ice cream |

3. Do I eat when I'm angry or bored?

4. Do I deny my body food to exercise control over myself?

Using the labels (a) through (e) given on the previous page, categorize each entry on your list. This will help you to recognize your reasons for and patterns of eating.

Think about your responses to the questions as you read further into this book. Write them down if you wish to do this exercise again at a later date and compare it with today's results. Also try to consider how your family influences the decisions you make about food.

# Parents Who Have the Best Intentions

The food awareness activity may have helped you discover why you eat what you do. The next step is learning the factors that may have influenced the way your parents taught you how to eat. Talk to your mother and/or father about their own upbringing—and ask them about the role that food played in their respective households. You may gain better understanding of their views about food once they've told you of their own experiences. For example, your father's family may have experienced a time when there wasn't enough to eat, which may explain why you have to clean your plate before you leave the dinner table. Your mother may have grown up in a household that encouraged dieting, which may help you understand why she watches everything you put in your mouth.

*Is your family's idea of a snack a pound of pasta?*

*Does your grandmother, when she looks after you, reward you with dessert after you've finished your homework?*

Part of growing up from adolescence to adulthood is learning how to express our feelings in an intelligent and understandable way. You want to speak to your parents in a manner that will encourage them to be responsive and supportive. This means being very specific about your concerns.

Ask them to respect your decisions, whether you decide to shop for/cook your own meals or follow a vegetarian (meatless) diet. This can be extremely difficult to do if the rules about food in your house are very rigid. Your family may not understand or respect your decisions about food. They may not want to make special considerations just for you.

It is important, however, not to attack your parents and tell them that their behavior is wrong. Making lifestyle adjustments is a learning process like any other—it requires consideration and patience. If you wish to involve your parents in creating a healthy household, you must also remember to respect their habits, routines, and personal preferences. It may be best to introduce small changes into your household to make it easier for everyone. Here are some suggestions for what you can do:

❑ Offer to cook for your family one night a week.

Offering to cook dinner for the family is a great way to introduce gradual changes in your family's eating habits.

- ❏ Ask family members what foods they like to eat and how they like the food prepared.
- ❏ Offer to help with the food shopping, and ask if you can make your own choices about some of the foods that are bought.
- ❏ If your family has rigid mealtimes, ask your parent(s) if the time can be varied a few days each week.

As you learn exciting new things about yourself, you may often be reminded by others that you're not yet an adult. It's difficult to make important decisions when they are monitored and sometimes even rejected by your mother and father. How do you prevent conflict from arising when you don't follow the examples set by your parents but choose other role models instead?

## Role Models

*Mirror, mirror on the wall. . .who am I? Can I become someone else? Who do I admire?*

A role model is a person in your life who shapes the way you see the world. As you become an adult, you adopt certain values or characteristics from people whom you admire. Maybe you've developed a sense of courage from learning about the fearless female pilot

Amelia Earhart. Or maybe you feel inspired by Anne Frank, the young Jewish girl who never doubted the power of love, even during a horrendous war against her people. Martin Luther King, Jr., the civil rights activist, endures as a role model for millions of African Americans.

In the home, we don't choose our role models; we are born with them. For young women, the mother is often their first role model. Young men often look to their father for approval and guidance. That is why our parents' approval can be so dangerously important to us. Sometimes the pressure to fulfill their expectations leaves us feeling guilty, anxious, or inadequate. Either we lead our lives trying to please them (with good grades, with our talents) or we shatter their expectations by deliberately misbehaving (getting in trouble at school, participating in illegal activities).

What are the reasons behind the way you act? Do you use food as a way to rebel against your parents or assert your independence? Sometimes young people may eat forbidden food or junk food outside the home as a way to express their autonomy. In this way, food becomes more than just fuel for the body. It can be a tool to use against our parents.

## Family Attitudes About Weight

*Mirror, mirror on the wall. . .am I beautiful? Am I overweight? What is my family's image of me?*

How does each of your parents discuss your appearance? Does your mother tell you that you're beautiful, or is she critical of your appearance? Does your father tease you about not being muscular, or is he proud of you just the way you are?

Earlier in this book, you were asked to determine what words about weight and appearance are spoken in your household. It's important to recognize your family's attitudes about these issues so that you can understand what shapes your eating habits. Your family is part of a world that encourages people to transform themselves into what society thinks is beautiful.

Constant conversation about physical appearance in your home inevitably affects the way you feel about your own image. Some parents who want their children to be happy believe that being thin and attractive will ensure that happiness. Parents may know from personal experience that overweight girls and boys are often shunned by society. How they choose to communicate these issues to you can either prevent or contribute to a lifelong preoccupation with your body.

Perhaps you think that your mother, the most important role model in your life, is more beautiful than you. If you see your mother drinking only coffee for breakfast and eating diet dinners, you may decide to follow her behavior. Or if you see your

Parents who carefully watch what their children eat may cause them to develop unhealthy relationships with food.

parents fussing over your sister's weight, you may find ways to get their attention by either overeating or starving yourself.

Since we have absolute control over our bodies, we may abuse ourselves in subtle (or not so subtle) ways to get attention, to make a point about who we are, or to rebel against what the rest of the world wants us to become. For a more detailed discussion of these matters, see chapter 5.

Sometimes it's not what your parents say, but what they don't say that has an effect on you. For example, you may decide to go on a diet to lose weight. If your parents don't say anything about it, you may see their silence as approval.

*When I was twelve, I decided to go on a diet. I guess I didn't think I needed to lose weight, but all my friends started taking diet pills and talking about how they wanted to be really thin. One day, while shopping with my mom, I bought a package of diet pills. She didn't say a word. I expected my mom to be shocked and tell me that I looked fine the way I was. When she didn't say anything, I decided I must be overweight because she obviously thought that the diet pills were a good idea.*

## The Media

*Mirror, mirror on the wall. . .who's the fairest of them all?*

What are the standards of beauty outside of the home? In American society, the message transmitted to us—through advertising, in the movies, on television, in magazines—is that to be beautiful is to be thin. Models are meant to wear clothes like hangers, flat and without wrinkles. Celebrities boast customized work-out routines with personal fitness trainers. Advertisements for diet programs promise personal success and happiness with weight loss. Even the physical appearance of high-profile lawyers, journalists, and politicians falls under public scrutiny.

Images of models and celebrities are everywhere. It's easy to see why people believe what models and celebrities look like is the norm, or standard for everyone else. But models' bodies are nothing like most people's. Their body-types are extreme in their proportions. It's important to understand that aspiring toward that ideal is impossible and unhealthy for most people.

Problems occur because our parents are affected by the media as well. They can unknowingly reinforce to you media messages about weight and body image .

## Body-Awareness Activity

Do you often read magazines such as *Seventeen, Teen, YM, Essence,* or *Sports Illustrated*? Here's a project for you to do by yourself or with a few friends. Sit down on the floor with a few sheets of paper, a pen, a pair of scissors, glue, and a pile of your

Magazines and advertisements send powerful messages about weight and body shape. It's easy to forget that these images portray only a very limited idea of beauty.

favorite magazines. If you need to use magazines that belong to family members, see if they are done reading them, since you will be cutting out pictures. If that is unacceptable for any reason, you could go to your local library and make copies of the pages you wish to use.

On a piece of paper, list five people in your life whom you consider to be role models. Write one sentence about why you chose each person.

Example:

1. Aunt Frieda              She is always kind, understanding, and helpful toward others.

2. Christopher Reeve        He leads an active, courageous life even though he is physically disabled.

3. Mrs. Crawford            She always manages to make learning about difficult subjects fun.

Now look in your magazines: Do any of the women or men in the advertisements look at all like

**MYTH:** Everyone could be thin if they had enough discipline.

**FACT:**
People's bodies are unique. It's impossible and dangerous for people to try to conform to the ideal of a very thin and/or muscular body.

anyone on your list? What does a "normal" person look like in these magazines?

Turn to the magazine's Table of Contents. How many times does the word "beauty" appear? Are there many headlines about how to look good or lose weight? Who are the subjects of the feature articles—were they interviewed because they're attractive and famous, or because they're smart, generous, or uniquely talented?

Cut out several pictures of women and men and paste them on a sheet of paper to design a collage. On the flip side of your paper, write down your ideas about how beauty is represented in magazines. Offer suggestions about how these attitudes could be altered by the media. For example:

*Models wear next to nothing in ads for cars, watches, shoes, and even food! Why not appeal to the people who actually buy these products for the reasons they buy them?*

*I purchased this magazine in Chinatown, but there are absolutely no Asian faces to be found in it. Match the magazine's content with its audience!*

After you (and/or your group of friends) have voiced your opinions on paper,  consider sending your work to one of the magazines from which you collected the images. People often use letter writing as a way to express their opinions. In our country, there is freedom of speech—and the more you exercise this right, the greater opportunity there is for change.

You might also consider sharing your opinions with your parents. Together, you can be aware of media messages and see how they affect what you think and feel about yourself. For further suggestions about how to generate awareness about weight obsession, see chapter 6.

# Weight Can Be a Family Affair:
## A Quick Lesson in Genetics

3

Now that you've spent some time looking at pictures of other people's bodies, let's take a closer look at your own. Do you ever wonder what makes our bodies so different from one another's?

*Why does Charice have such long legs?*

*How is it that Karen wears a size 36C bra and I barely fill out a 32A?*

*Why do some boys have more defined muscles than others?*

There are many fac-tors that

determine body shape and weight, including eating habits, energy output (the amount of exercise you do), and—most important and often most misunderstood—genetics. What many people fail to realize is that we inherit our body shapes and sizes from our parents. Genetics is the strongest factor—more than how much we eat and how often we exercise—in determining what we look like.

## What Is a Gene?

Genes are units within the chromosomes of cells that make up our bodies. Genes are responsible for producing traits that run in our families. This fact was discovered by an Austrian monk named Gregor Mendel. The study of genetics involves the reasons certain traits are passed from one generation to the next. Much of your physical appearance comes from your parents. Each person's body weight and shape, like his or her intelligence or personality, are unique; no two people are exactly the same. What we learn from the laws of genetics is that each one of us is a special combination of our parents' traits.

## So How Do Genes Work?

To understand how genes work, we'll look at how they determine whether we are male or female. The egg of the female reproductive system and the sperm of the male reproductive system have twenty-three chromosomes each. When the egg and sperm join at fertilization, they make a cell with forty-six chromosomes. The cells multiply and develop into a human being. All human cells have forty-six chromosomes. This process lets one gene from the father combine with one gene from the mother for each trait.

This is also how the sex of a person is determined. The mother's gene contributes a pair of chromosomes. In females, the chromosomes are the same, or XX. That is because the egg produces only X chromosomes. The father's gene also contributes a pair of chromosomes. In males, the chromosomes are different, or XY. That is because half of the male's sperm contributes an X chromosome and the other half contributes a Y chromosome.

If an X-chromosome sperm fertilizes the egg, it produces a female. If a Y chromosome sperm fertilizes the egg, it produces a male.

The same process occurs to determine weight and body shape. In other words, both parents contribute

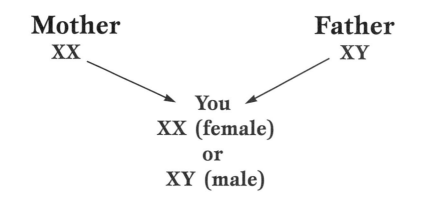

their genes. These genes then combine to produce a new and unique person: You!

Trying to change your body's configuration is like dying your hair—no matter what shade you apply, the roots will still grow back in their natural color. What is a natural (and healthy) weight for each person differs. It is because of our genes that this "set point" weight range is established. Some people are simply destined to be heavier or lighter than others.

## Dangers of Dieting

Eating habits and exercise control your weight and body shape to some extent. But it can be extremely dangerous and discouraging to go on and off of strict diets and exercise routines because a portion—or all—of the weight lost is eventually gained back. This kind of yo-yo dieting can hurt more than it helps. This is because the brain recognizes what the body's set-point should be. When we eat less food,

Teens may engage in unhealthy weight management practices, such as taking diet pills, that can put them at risk for illness.

our bodies compensate for the lost calories (measurements of the energy in food) by lowering our metabolism (the rate at which the food we eat is processed). Thus, dieting can actually promote weight gain because our bodies act to retain what little food we put in them.

Dieting has many harmful effects. A lack of food can cause you to feel light-headed and tired. You may experience nausea or stomach pain. Dieting can be especially harmful to teenagers, whose bodies are still growing and need to get all the proper nutrients for their development. Nutrients ensure that the body grows and functions properly.

Diets can also affect you psychologically, making you depressed, irritable, and moody. You may experience these feelings because you are depriving yourself of food or because you are not losing as much weight as you wanted. Overall, diets promote unhealthy eating habits and unhealthy relationships with food. In the worst cases, diets may lead to serious eating disorders. Studies show that 80 percent of eating disorders began with dieting.

# What Exactly Is an Eating Disorder?

4

When we rebel against our set-point weight and try desperately to lose body fat, we are obsessed with food and give in to the false and impossible standards set for us by others. Remember the activity you did in chapter 2 about role models? Some women and men use the standards set in fashion magazines, Hollywood, and other high-profile venues to determine whether and how they measure up to what's "beautiful." If people feel they do not measure up, they may develop very unhealthy attitudes and behaviors in an attempt to achieve these unrealistic and limited beauty standards.

Sometimes people develop eating disorders because of family problems. Their home lives may be unstable because parents divorce or the family moves several times. If parents don't let a child learn to make personal decisions, a child may respond by taking control over his or her body in a destructive way.

While eating disorders usually affect females, an increasing number of males are developing them as well. Currently, over 8 million Americans suffer from eating disorders. One million are male. Eating disorders include anorexia nervosa, bulimia nervosa, and binge eating disorder (also known as compulsive eating). Compulsive exercise is considered a related eating disorder problem. A person can suffer from one or any combination of the four. Each disorder has certain characteristics, but they all present very dangerous health risks. The reasons why a person develops an eating disorder are complex and varied.

An eating disorder involves a person's eating habits and his or her attitudes about weight, food, and body shape, along with other psychological factors. People with eating disorders may experience problems in their job, school, or personal relationships. They may be distrustful of other people and isolate themselves. They may feel out of control of their lives. Eating disorders are symptoms of these problems.

It's important to understand why and how an eating disorder happens. By doing so, you can help yourself or someone you love. The sooner an eating disorder is identified, the sooner it can be treated.

*A high school A-student, Jessica never believed she was pretty until she started dieting—and became extremely underweight. Jessica developed unusual eating rituals, including weighing her food, cutting solids into tiny pieces, and carrying a head of lettuce in her backpack. Her menstrual periods stopped entirely, and she became very weak.*

*At first, Jessica's friends congratulated her for her willpower to lose weight. But soon they began to worry, as did her teachers and family. Jessica was terrified of gaining back the pounds she had worked so hard to lose. She refused to admit she had a problem. Then Jessica collapsed at school one day and was taken to the hospital. There she began treatment for her eating disorder. It took several hospitalizations and a good deal of individual and family therapy for Jessica to face—and deal with—her problems.*

For Jessica, food and weight had become obsessions, which the medical community identifies as symptoms of eating disorders. One thing to note is that a person with an eating disorder may have symptoms of more than one disorder.

## Anorexia Nervosa

People who intentionally starve themselves suffer from anorexia nervosa (which literally means "nervous lack of appetite"). This disorder involves extreme weight loss, causing a person to be at least 15 percent below the healthy weight for his or her body. Many of its victims look emaciated but are still convinced they are overweight. They are so obsessed with losing weight that they ignore the body's hunger signals. Many of them must be hospitalized to prevent death from starvation.

People with anorexia often suffer from painful stomach cramps as their bodies try to retain any and all available nutrition. Starvation lowers the blood pressure and makes the heart rate slow and weak. A female with anorexia loses estrogen (the female hormone), which causes the bones to lose mass and weaken. This can cause osteoporosis. A male with anorexia loses testosterone (the male hormone), which results in decreased sexual desire. Dehydration from loss of fluids can cause an electrolyte imbalance that can result in death.

## Bulimia Nervosa

Bulimia nervosa literally means "ox hunger." This disorder is characterized by a self-defeating cycle of bingeing (consuming of a large amount of food in a short time) and purging. A purge is the act of voiding food to prevent weight gain. The most common forms of purging are self-induced vomiting, rigorous exercise, and the use of drugs that induce vomiting or bring on bowel movements.

A person with bulimia can develop ulcers, which are holes or tears in the mouth, stomach, and/or throat. This is because the stomach acid used to digest food is continually brought up through vomiting. A person with bulimia may also have painful stomach cramps from severe constipation and become very weak. Bulimia can also cause electrolyte imbalance.

## Binge Eating Disorder

People who have binge eating disorder consume large portions of food in small periods of time (as people with bulimia would do) but do not purge. They often eat when they are not hungry and keep eating long after they feel full. People with binge eating disorder use food as a way to deal with uncomfortable feelings, such as anger, loneliness, and fear. Thus, they may become overweight or suffer from obesity.

When people become addicted to exercise, they become obsessed with working out and losing weight.

## Compulsive Exercise

Compulsive exercise is an eating disorder-related problem in which a person uses exercise to get rid of calories. It is also known as exercise bulimia because the person is using exercise to purge food from his or her body. A person who exercises compulsively feels the need to work out, not because he or she wants to, but because he or she has to. The body may develop painful injuries, such as stress fractures and torn muscles. Because a compulsive exerciser burns more calories than he or she takes in, the body breaks down and becomes very weak.

## Common Warning Signs of Eating Disorders

- ❑ Analyzing the size and shape of your body all the time
- ❑ Thinking about your weight all the time and constantly weighing yourself
- ❑ Constantly thinking about food, cooking, and eating
- ❑ Eating only certain foods in specific amounts
- ❑ Feeling uncomfortable about or while eating around other people
- ❑ Taking diet pills or laxatives
- ❑ Feeling that you should exercise more no matter how much you exercise
- ❑ Not feeling good about yourself unless you are thin—but never being satisfied with how thin you are
- ❑ Forcing yourself to throw up
- ❑ Purposely losing lots of weight very quickly
- ❑ Stopping of menstrual periods

You don't have to have every symptom on this list to be at risk. If these symptoms are familiar to you, please consider getting help. Recovering from an eating disorder can be a long and difficult process.

A person needing treatment may be hospitalized or admitted to an in-patient program, where he or she lives while being treated. Often, individual therapy and group therapy are essential in helping a person to recover.

**MYTH:**

Eating disorders affect only white, middle-class females.

**FACT:**

Eating disorders are prevalent among women and men (usually between the ages of 11 and 30) of any socioeconomic class, race, or intelligence level.

There are many organizations, support groups, and resources devoted entirely to eating disorder treatment and prevention. Help is available to those who need it and want it. Recovery is a tough road to take, but well worth taking. Many young men and women have recovered. If you are male, you may feel too shy to ask for help. But remember that you are not alone. It's important to ask for help. In the end, treatment will save your life.

Talking with a friend who may be suffering from an eating disorder can give her the support she needs when she's ready to ask for help.

## What Can I Do if Someone I Know Is Silently Suffering?

It's not easy to confront family members or friends about problems. You may be unsure if you should say anything at all. However, if you observe behavior indicating that someone you care about has an eating disorder, there are a few things you can do—and a few things you shouldn't do.

| DO | DON'T |
|---|---|
| 1 Speak to the person privately. | 1 Speak to an adult without first talking to the person who you suspect has an eating disorder (unless the situation is an absolute emergency*). |
| 2 Calmly tell the person the specific observations that have caused your concern. | 2 Confront the person in a group of people and fire accusations. |
| 3 Suggest that the person be evaluated by someone who understands eating disorders (school nurse, guidance counselor, parent, teacher). | 3 Categorize the person's behavior as wrong, crazy, sick, or stupid. |
| 4 Allow the person time to respond. Listen carefully and nonjudgmentally. | 4 Promise to keep what you have observed a secret. (Telling the person that he/she can trust you should not imply that you will sit back and watch your friend self-destruct.) |

* What is an absolute emergency? If the person loses consciousness, vomits blood, experiences heart failure, is in a state of delirium, or is clearly suicidal.

43

# Suggestions for Healthy Living

5

True, the fewer processed foods we eat, the more likely we are to get the nutrients (natural vitamins and minerals in whole foods) we need. But it is not correct to assume that a healthy diet can be maintained by cutting back on our meals. As we have already learned, our bodies are a lot like cars: they need fuel and can't function without good nutrition.

The amount of energy we need from food varies depending on our age, our lifestyle, and our activities.During childhood and adolescence, our energy requirements are very high because we are still growing. As we get older, our bodies begin to slow down. But at all stages of development, it is important to eat enough healthy food to prevent various diseases from developing later in life.

Parents, teachers, friends, coaches, doctors, dietitians, the U.S. Department of Health (government organization that monitors the distribution of food in the United States)—all have their own ideas of what "good" food is.

Earlier in this book, you were asked to keep a food journal to observe your personal reasons for eating the foods you do. Now perhaps you will consider eating certain foods because they are better for your body.

## Activity

What exactly is in the food you eat?

List your favorite foods and write down their main ingredients.

Do these ingredients give your body a proper balance of vitamins and minerals?

How does the food you eat make your body feel?

For example:

| Food | Ingredients |
|------|-------------|
| french fries | potato, oil |
| pizza | dough, cheese, tomato |
| chocolate bar | chocolate, sugar |
| soda | carbonated water, sugar |

Now, think about healthy alternatives to your favorite foods. You could grill a sandwich of bread, cheese, and fresh tomatoes instead of having a slice of pizza. If you get a sugar high from a candy bar, why not have a piece of melon in its place, which would also provide water and vitamins, and give you some real energy.

Parents and teachers may refer to items in the above list as junk food, which usually indicates brand-name food that is either highly processed or contains high levels of sugar and salt. A good way to keep a well-balanced diet is to look at the list of ingredients on the package. Almost every food item in the market now contains a detailed breakdown of ingredients—including vitamins, proteins, and fats—that are important for good nutrition.

Overall, the most important thing to remember is that eating right is good for your body. Good food makes you feel better, gives you more energy, helps you get restful sleep, and keeps your body functioning well. That doesn't mean you can never have any foods containing sugar, salt, or caffeine. Most registered dietitians will tell you that it's a matter of moderation. A balanced diet is a flexible one. It doesn't put anything completely off limits. But you'd be surprised how much better you feel when you eat foods that are filled with vitamins and nutrients!

## Exercise Makes the Heart Beat Faster . . . and Longer

Of course, putting good food in your mouth is only one part of nourishing yourself. You need to be active to help pump blood throughout your body. Exercise gives you energy, makes you more confident, and helps you sleep better. It also strengthens your heart, improves circulation, and keeps your muscles and bones strong and healthy. Regular exercise will help prevent heart disease and osteoporosis. Again, though, moderation is the key.

### Make Exercise Fun

When you make exercise enjoyable, not something you do to lose weight, you are more likely to stick

with it. You can become frustrated and discouraged about exercising if you are using it to lose weight. When you don't see results right away, you may give it up altogether. But exercise has so many other benefits. First, it releases endorphins, which are the body's natural painkillers and automatically make you feel good. Exercise gives you energy and makes you feel more comfortable in your body. It reduces stress and makes you feel self-confident and ready to take on exciting, new challenges.

Moderate exercise is great for the body and mind. Jogging, walking, dancing, or anything else that increases the heart rate will keep the body running smoothly.

## What Is the Right Amount of Exercise?

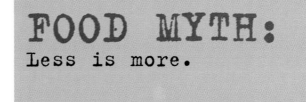

According to the Centers for Disease Control (CDC) and the American Council on Sports Medicine, it is recommended that you get "about thirty minutes of moderate exercise on most days of the week." Michael Pratt, the physical activity coordinator for the CDC says that doesn't mean you should go to extremes. In fact, exercise can get out of hand, as we learned earlier, in the form of compulsive exercise. The whole idea is that you should enjoy physical activity. It should not be a chore, and you should not become obsessed with it.

## What Kind of Exercise Is Right for Me?

You may try many types of activity before you find what you like. You can do different things on different days. The important thing is to find what you like. That can mean taking a bike ride or going hiking with friends. It can mean a brisk walk in the morning, or going dancing in a club at night. You could help your family by cleaning up around your house or apartment. You could join a sport team at school or start one of your own. If you like to rollerblade, start a street-hockey team. Offer to

Exercise merely means moving the body and making the heart beat faster, which can be accomplished by a vast number of activities.

coach your younger sister's soccer team. In other words, as long as you're moving, you can do anything you want. If you use exercise to have fun and stay healthy rather than to lose weight, you'll feel more satisfied with what you've done.

PLEASE REMEMBER: Exercise is for the joy of feeling your body move and function effectively, not just to purge fat or burn calories. Compulsive exercise, like compulsive eating, can lead to addiction. If you consistently work out to the point of becoming faint, or if you schedule all of your free time around physical activity (mostly by yourself and not in groups or on teams), you may need to seek professional help to restructure your habits.

# Generating Awareness About Weight Issues

6

It is hoped that you have learned from the facts, scenarios, and activities in this book that there is no one formula for perfection or beauty. But it's not easy to combat all the different messages you get from your family and the media. It's tough being a teenager. Our parents know it. So do Hollywood executives and magazine editors. But no one knows better what challenges teens face than you yourself do—and your voice can and should be heard. There are a variety of ways to communicate your feelings and opinions to other people. Here are some suggestions.

## Your Parents

- ❑ Sit down and talk honestly with your parents about what you think and feel. They may not even be aware of how critical they seem to you. This will also give them a chance to apologize or explain if their words and actions have been misunderstood by you.

- ❑ If you think that talking to your parents about your eating concerns is too difficult, perhaps a letter to them would allow you to express your feelings in a clear, uninterrupted way.

- ❑ Try speaking with a counselor about how you feel, or ask a registered dietician for suggestions about incorporating changes into your family's food choices. The American Dietetic Association has a hot line that can answer any questions you may have about good nutrition.

## School

- ❑ Are you criticized about your body by

**Open and honest communication between parents and children can be extremely helpful in preventing the onset of an eating disorder.**

school gym teachers or professionals? Circulate a petition (a letter with signatures of others who feel the same way as you do) for change.

◻ Start a support group with classmates that meets to discuss issues such as body image and self-esteem.

## The Media

◻ Tired of television shows and commercials promoting the same beauty ideal? Write letters to the network representatives. Many stations also have email addresses where you can send your comments. The same method works for the magazines you read. Write a letter to the editor. It might be printed and your message would be read by thousands of people.

❐ If you are looking for better role models on television and in the movies, don't watch programs or buy advertised products that promote impossible body ideals. Put your money and your time into shows and products that promote positive self-image.

Generating awareness on your own will help you develop your own identity. That means having your own thoughts and ideas that may be different from those of your friends and your parents. It can be especially important if your parents continue to have unhealthy attitudes about food and weight. You may not be able to change their minds. Still you do have control over your eating habits and what you think about your body. Making your own choices and decisions will help distance you from any negative influences in your life.

Remember, this world is an interesting place because of the people in it. Your worth is not based on your looks but on who you are as a person. Celebrate your diversity!

# Glossary

**adolescence**  Youth; pre-teen and teenage years of a person's life.

**autonomy**  Independence; the ability to make your own decisions.

**chromosomes**  The DNA-containing bodies that have all or most of the genes of an individual.

**diverse**  Having different elements; varied.

**electrolyte imbalance**  A life-threatening condition in which a person has little of the minerals the body needs to be healthy.

**estrogen**  The female hormone that is responsible for feminine characteristics of the human body.

**genes** Units within the chromosomes that are responsible for producing traits that run in families.

**metabolism**  The process by which the body turns food into energy.

**nutrient** Vitamins, minerals, and other food ingredients that your body requires in order to stay healthy.

**osteoporosis** A disease characterized by a decrease in bone mass, causing bones to weaken and break easily.

**role model** A person you admire for what he or she has done in life.

**self-destructive** Hurting yourself.

**set point** The weight your body naturally tends to be when you eat and exercise normally.

**testosterone** The male hormone that is responsible for masculine characteristics of the human body.

**yo-yo dieting** Going on and off a diet, constantly losing and regaining weight.

# Where to Go
# for Help

**American Dietetic Association**
216 West Jackson Boulevard, Suite 805
Chicago, IL 60606
(312) 899-0040
Nutrition hotline: (800) 366-1655
Web site: http://www.eatright.org

**Anorexia Nervosa and Related Eating Disorders, Inc. (ANRED)**
P.O. Box 5102
Eugene, OR 97405
(541) 344-1144
Web site: http://www.anred.com

**Eating Disorders Awareness and Prevention, Inc. (EDAP)**
603 Stewart Street, Suite 803
Seattle, WA 98101
(206) 382-3587
Web site: http://members.aol.com/edapinc

**Gürze Books**
P.O. Box 2238
Carlsbad, CA 92018-9883
(800) 756-7533
Web site: http://www.gurze.com
Gürze books is a publisher that specializes in books on eating disorders. You can order their books directly. The books will be shipped in a plain, confidential package.

**National Association of Anorexia Nervosa and Associated Disorders (ANAD)**
Box 7
Highland Park, IL 60035
(847) 432-8000 ext. 5728
Web site: http://members.aol.com/ anad20/index.html

**National Eating Disorders Organization (NEDO)**
6655 South Yale Avenue
Tulsa, OK 74136
(918) 481-4044
Web site: http://www.laureate.com

**Overeaters Anonymous Headquarters**
P.O. Box 44020
Rio Rancho, NM 87174-4020
(505) 891-2664
Web site: http://www.overeatersanonymous.org

# In Canada

**Anorexia Nervosa and Associated Disorders (ANAD)**
109 - 2040 West 12th Avenue
Vancouver, BC V6J 2G2
(604) 739-2070

**The National Eating Disorders Information Centre**
College Wing, 1st Floor, Room 211
200 Elizabeth Street
Toronto, ON M5G 2C4
(416) 340-4156

# For Further Reading

Berry, Joy. *Good Answers to Tough Questions About Weight Problems and Eating Disorders.* Chicago: Children's Press, 1990.

Cooke, Kaz. *Real Gorgeous: The Truth About Body and Beauty.* New York: W. W. Norton, 1996.

Crook, Marion. *Looking Good: Teenagers and Eating Disorders.* Toronto: NC Press, Ltd., 1992.

Folkers, Gladys, and Jeanne Engelman. *Taking Charge of My Mind and Body: A Girls' Guide to Outsmarting Alcohol, Drugs, Smoking and Eating Problems.* Minneapolis: Free Spirit Publishing, 1997.

Kolodny, Nancy J. *When Food's a Foe: How You Can Confront and Conquer Your Eating Disorder.* New York: Little, Brown and Company, 1992.

McCoy, Kathy, and Wibblesman, Charles. *The New Teenage Body Book.* New York: The Body Press/Perigee Books, 1992.

Packer, Alex J. *Bringing Up Parents.* Minneapolis: Free Spirit, 1993.

# Index

**H**
happiness, 6, 21, 24
Health, Department of, 45
health/fitness, 23-24, 44-45, 47, 50, 55
heart disease, 47
hospitalization, 36, 37, 41
hunger, 10, 37, 38

**I**
ideal body, 24, 55

**L**
laxatives, 38, 40

**M**
media, 23-24, 27, 52, 54-55
menstruation, 36, 40
metabolism, 32
models, 23-24, 27

**N**
nourishment, 7
nutrients/nutrition, 7, 33, 37, 44, 46-47, 53

**O**
obesity, 38
osteoporosis, 37, 47
overeating, 12, 22

**P**
parents, 6, 7, 8, 10, 12-13, 16-19, 20, 21-23, 24, 27, 29, 31, 35, 52-53, 55
  intentions of, 16-27
pressure, family, 6, 20

**P**
punishment, 9, 14
purging, 7, 38, 39, 51

**R**
race, 6
reproductive system, 29-30
role models, 19-20, 21, 25, 34, 55

**S**
self-abuse, 22
self-esteem/self-confidence, 6, 47-48, 54
self-image, 7, 21, 55
set point, 31, 32, 34
society, influence of, 21, 23
starvation, 12, 22, 37
support, parental, 6, 17
support groups, 41, 54

**T**
testosterone, 37
therapy, 36, 41
traditions, family 6

**V**
values, 6, 19
vegetarian diet, 17
vomiting, 38, 40

**W**
weight obsession, 27, 34, 37, 40

**Y**
yo-yo dieting, 31-32

## About The Author

Elizabeth Frankenberger is a freelance writer living in New York City.

## Design and Layout by Christine Innamorato

## Consulting Editor: Michele I. Drohan

## Photo Credits

Photo on p.11 by Jeffrey Mark Dunn/Viesti Associates, Inc.: pgs. 48, 50 by Skjold Photography; All other photos by John Bentham.